Milford

Evan R. Underbrink

VITALITY buzz, bliss + books
Cincinnati, OH

This book is dedicated to Curtis Gatley,
who brought me into the living world of poetry,
and listened to my first real poem.
Thank you, friend, for Spokane.

in gratitude to the VATRONS
who pre-ordered and breathed life into this book

Jason Bixman, Michelle Blevins, Helen Buswinka
Tyler Crane, Stewart Delo, Denise & Mike Eck
Matthew Edholm, Kyle Elliott, Karen Finch
Marie Hawley, Scott Holland, David Jaeger
Lisa Marie Koury Parker, Tonya Lawrence
Alexander Markham, Moisey Mikheyev
Stefany Oliva, Steven Petersheim, Brittany Rabidue
Kirstin Rose-Bean, Melissa Rowland, Alison Sabean
Angie Scholl, Lea Sevey, Caitlyn Shipp
Brian Shircliff, Kendrick Sullivan, Erin Underbrink
Lucas Underbrink, Thomas Underbrink, Vern Walker
Caroline Wiseman, Nickolas Woll

CONTENTS

Preface

Many good things in life are begun when something you love meets something you need. The best things are begun when what you love and need sparks something in others as well. This book began with a resolution, and a hope, to accomplish all three. If you are reading this, I feel rather safe in assuming you enjoy words. Perhaps you are also like me in thinking that words and food go together: after all, we taste both. Words can be sweet and tangy like raspberries, or hold the distinct bittersweetness of heartbreak and dark chocolate.

Every poem in this book, except one, was written while I lived for a year at the Jesuit Spiritual Center in Milford, Ohio. Surrounded by woods, groundhogs, and quite a bit of time in between running spiritual retreats for teenagers, I immersed myself in practices of spiritual meditation and prayer, I learned how better to speak in the midst of discernment, I lived in intentional community, in regrets, love, breakup, joy, anger, sorrow, peace; in other words, I had time enough to write about a year of life in retreat. In this context, I made two simple resolutions: to cook more, and to write a book. Here is the book.

Amidst all the ways life tugs at our sleeve and whispers us awake at night: work, family, finances, and the endless demands of screens, taking the better part of a year off for contemplation may be impossible for most. If that is your case, I wrote this book for you. Perhaps coming alongside my own life through these writings, you may find moments of that sense of intimacy, thoughtfulness, and spiritual insight which accompanies time lived in retreat. You may, then again, be the sort of person who has or is going for extended times of spiritual reflection. I rush to celebrate with you in these words. Perhaps you will find within them something of your own experience, that we might share in God together.

I can only further say thank you for letting this text be a companion to you, wherever you are. Words are capsules of life, little pocket dimensions where you, dear, wonderful, mysterious you, and I are allowed to share some precious talk across time. This space is sacred to me; thank you, for spending time in it. All else that I have to say in prefatory matters can be found within the first poem of this collection, *Apology*. For this reason, I shall leave it here and invite you to find what meaning you can on your own in the poems that follow.

Evan R. Underbrink
April 2022

Apology

Some of these in here are
good. Most of those
on whom I've imposed
them, agree.

I have left the bad ones
in, because
this is a book about a life
I share with those
who let me
impose, like you,
you see.

This book is a room
in the basement of a church, where
a friar sets his wood to whittle.
Here there be splinters
chips, knots, tears,
the scent of stale beer,
and once in a whiled wood, whiled page, wiled day,
a glimpse, if in sketch,
of God.

Reorientation

I accept you
Broad world
windowless to words, doorless, yet I accept you
in the falling of the sparrow
In the curve of a car
From whence do each come?
In truth I know little; in truth
not.

Stretch, stretch, cries the common soul
or is it only my soul? In my world so little
so much to me.

Look you, reader, look
Could I but hold a seed from my wilderwood
In your hearts, with St. Kevin hands
on such delicate eggs as feeling,
wait for them to break shells, sprout,
Then Pilate would prove the prophet
and the world turn turvy tops-
stop, stop, and in the word spirants
breathe

You may call it play, word play, the shudder of a soul
at the sound of airplanes
at the automation of a garage door
the quest for a word, a word
a word
Patoo, patoo, tohoo-wee
the birdsong in morning twilight before light.

I accept that I will not know
you not to know I, nor I you
in that soul place, the soul to soul space,
the end of desire being the ritual of its evocation
the end for me only begun for you,
begin believe

Or let my nephesh perish in swirls of escaping time
Ungrieved

The Hour Before I lost You

Silver-sliver,
trickle tongue down lolling
touch brings the shiver;
this fireworks of flesh
unwrapping the wanting,
wanting.

Perspire.

Clothes puddles
predicts the reign
just enough time- breathe
think oh, oh,
I am the thunder god
here in the stardust of skin made to fit my bolts, and
that I should have remembered my
umbrella.

Then lips, tongue, twist
Flesh flutter touch
Thrust.

A little laugh at the
engineering of these things
there, right there,
fishing for the phrases falls to
there, there, oh

And then I am cold
Myself again, soaked. you
hold on long enough
for me to know You
(are already gone)

A Sparrow

Alight! A sparrow on my soul
is nothing too pretensive
is nothing over bold.

The gentle wave
of ruffled wings
prickle-pecked minds which
daily fly and fade.

Yet love is in the sparrow's wing
counted by God lest it fall.
See it flutter, fail,
yet with a laugh tilt at tomorrow and
it being Fall, nestle,
into my chest to sleep.

Hold Love Within the Mind

Hold "Love" within the mind,
let it sing.
Invoke the name in memory,
so summoned, let its hour be sweet.

Sweeter still the love imperished
beyond time, ever now,
clamored joy in quiet call
simple peace in particular-mad everything.

Love is Lord in a many kingdomed court,
wherever hearts beat for more than self.
He promenades past the rich, who sell his appearing,
and find not much in the timed whirl of stars.

A king who thiefly sneaks to
tweak the nose of
working folk in factory rows,
tickle beards of broad waisted bachelor bucks.

As if to say, here is love,
and love begins before all beginnings
at home in everything, wishing
all to be its home.

To

To see the snow as a million-diamoned gift
made more rare, not less
that it stays only for its own brilliance,
denying coveting grasps its beauty
giving greedy hands only humble water;

to feel within the silken sheet
the deathbeds of each worm
whose life we gave
to account beauty's charge;

to dream, and with a dream to know
the import of your own worst shadow,
yet know still to still the soul
by claiming what was left in restless graved
memory;

To be such as one as any such
Ones would speak of such a one
Yet know that you are you,

is to be the majesty of self,
and in a royal self to
rule the inner place
greater than the world.

Phantasm

I.

What is it to lie?
He asked his empty pockets,
and found them full.
He lied a thousand dreamy faces,
before the first came tumbling true,
by this a world of phantasm embraces,
took him to fill its highest womb.

He saw the horse that flies
from faithful spires of sandy dunes,
where sings the song of hallowed wise,
who hope for heaven's late arrive.

He loosed his limbs on longing
Lengths of jaw-dropped open loving
At last feeling a hunger shaking
Upon a spine full well sated.

He wept upon the Lie's lasting threshold
Found fate who dawdles but does not fail,
And saw the liars hour growing hollow
Felt his fancies growing pale.

II.

So then arrived the question looming,
Is face of king who came up booming:
Am I lie's last leap in darkness,
Or truth Incarnate to dispel the gloom?

Choose, choose, but beware the liar
For in him only his great doom
While honest men are met with mercy
The liar forces backwards nature
So ends at last alone entombed.

The world is pregnant
in its secret places, bump
the wild writhing of leg, limb
hook, tooth claw
hand?

Am I so able to step outside
the machine of my own creation?
Can I with trembling simian rooks
grip upon too-straight lines?

III.
Yet to kiss, hip sway
stretch tip taste in twilights and tide turns
this the envy of angels
the pleasures of peoples

I take all of me
Love, and learning love
in the wrinkle fold liver-spotted
time we are left.
To know, and know,
and at last in the pregnant nature,
Go.

Requiem for the Classroom

Of the songs of Marathon
no lyre plays the lay, no lyre
in the learner's tomb, where
wine-blooded Homer decays.
What cants are here
to empress young hearts
within the mused arts
to bring the living strains?
The eye, glutton octopus
Has wrested ear from all its reign
So Grendel weeps not for want of arms,
But for the cage of inky stains.

Give out the old songs!
Let them sing upon the mind
you choicest words to batten me, of shepherds
and lovers from rare ould times.
Laurel the teller, warm his bread
away the cameras off to bed,
let King Story take his fresh domain!
to stroll through sound
to hearts complex and plain.

Then sing of new songs!
Tales wrought to spite machine unlife,
full brimmed of darkened screens,
split atoms, loss of time
For taking toast and tea.
Let them be sung, swung
in their greatest notes
bring us in, back
to the festal ecstasy of
You, hypocrite lecteur, and me.

Break Fade

It was true that things
are in their fading time as we
became each other's history.
But in the fade, what things were there?
Let me touch them once
more:

A modest little mansion,
Castle enough, with two baths and
a room fretted with glow in the dark stars we called —
no, we never did find a name for it
never found the
time.

The rooms grew dark with dust
shapeless gray, cracking walls to
let in the bitter fights. Seems
trite, but for one glimmer
(Quick!)
Gone moment I thought, I
might have found
more than a place to sleep.

It was a damn shame I wrote
no poetry for you (lips
too busy kissing art)
only this empty suitcase of
Lines, waiting
to be packed up.
It was a damn -

We found no love at the bottom of our wanting.
Only empty rooms and

two beaten hearts.
Time one was
gone.

Giving Blood

Giving blood was the least of my offenses
said the king of pallid
skin and lonely time before the screen,
his cloak a tatter of spider silk
such was my fated future.
Until -

Until nothing. The king deposed, yes but
By a queen not so thirsty yet
more glutted, desire.
All the robes were gone then
turned to the blight of ceremony.
And yet -

The same. The revolving clockwork of
ages aged her, so here republic ruined in divorcing
birthed a republic of ambition, growing
growing fast and eaten by revolution by
little heart-lords who quibble themselves into bureaucrats
so republics can court
my soul to inaction.

...

Hope
Is the king who stays
Upon a wheeled regal throne.
Teases great men to better
selves, good men to deeper
Love, hails sharply on the sinner's
Soul,
Who lords upon a grander stage,
trades his weal with all the world.
In hope we have our future.
In hope we find our way.

Infatuation

She was the queen of
unexpectation, fairy
fey love bold
bright there
gone.
Mete in life, might
be the meeting of such a —
but at the bottom just a simple soul.

I love the surface of things,
where imagination holds
banquet with Being, and his twin brother
Becoming.

She became the lady at my center self
and being so,
was lost.
The image possible, or
woman real?
Either? Both?
I go on, by all roads, unexpectedly
Alone.

Gym

It was never about the weights
sweat drip skin stretch inner
scream, cant can't
No.
Never about the weights.

For the worst hour, it was about
the mirrors, sniper
focus on the folds
pound less, ego add
pound ego -
No, at bottom
not about the mirrors.

The air pressed in
cherished like a dying breed
fed veins, quivering, coming
to their best being.
I free to breath one fleeing gulp of
mastery, before
the next rep.
And the next

Burn

What do you run on
when you run on empty?

Snapshot quick trick to the bullshit get
up this ain't no practice spar days dirk-strike, dodge-
Where are you?
Look, look now before the moment is

Empty?

There is no such thing.
Something always burns
if only the self.

Wherein I Yell at Marketing

I never found the truth in
Advertising, screen on screen
the mechanics seen in their ecstasy, why
sell an endorphin that
was never yours? Simulacra
where does the money come from
that I know behind the vision sold
makes your job work?

Alas I know all your talk is
Preparation and bubbles, the Coke
Is not Christmas in June, but never
Just sugar water.

Thank you for selling me pleasure
it is still not yours, but
was never mine either.
It was nice to see the pretty girls dance
next to your product, and pretend I
belonged, in
a belonging that never was.

Wherein I Howl at Husserl

I live with bifocal interest
between the thing that is,
And the is it means.

Upon the blinded eye falls stark
tables — no that is the interpretation.
Brown. Object. Matter?
White sheets — too imagistic.
White this. This! You see.
Zu den Sachen selbst

Upon the other open Odin eye
to be is a many-meaning thing:
sheets are sails on desks a dream's
inspiration breathed to carpenter's hands
Furnishings.

To be among the learned is to hear
a thousand voices daily crying,
"cast out the eye which causeth"
no, not sin, but less clear vision of things.
For I do not see half so clear
the is
for its meanings mar
manifold meanings, for
one is a stigma to the other.

Blind Old Ed shuffles by, chuckles
Plato tilts at caves, for
the wise know they name
what is, and being is, is more
by having name.

Staying, Holding, Hoping

I've fallen in love with the fight, even
Though I lose every time.
Staying, holding, hoping.
Symbols crowd in, making
their sense of it all:
The boxer on
the ropes breath
short, eyes
shot.
c'mon then hit
me again.
Again.
The gambler on
His last twenty making
promises but no
Recovery.
The soldier vomits in
dirt, cover
it keep
up the PT. Don't think duck then-
The farmer watches his
apple tree, maybe
next year the buds
will grow plump with their promised
purpose and
the crows will not have all their
fill.
Staying, holding, hoping
Tied to our dreams.

The Howl

Not enough in me to cry
these days, so I
write. I
wish I could
Sing.

These bones throb with
Pagliacci, the rising
bars the loss of

Here is a little makeup, paint
me in satin blues, strip
then clothe me in the tear filled
Ocean, let the paint bleed
out like children's chalk.

With it, I go too.

Sunday at 3pm

I am littered about my room,
unspooled before you, between
run down shoes and stained
coats asking how did I get this
Way?

The pause is always answer
Enough.

Time is the baron of pregnant
(Meaning. Time)
to pick, to know
what could be done. To reveal
the perfection of having done, and
find more to do.

Departures

I leave behind myself
Wholly, yet in the moments that become
only dates
in the places I have been.

I am not sad, not
often but oh
so intensely, when
I see myself go.
The new thing,
Me, unstable,
fixed, in full

                  quivering

                                potential,

like always before
before

I learn to love the

                          ink

while fresh and so easy to
smudge.

                            Then

it dries and I

must adore the next

(splotch

—

—

moment when you
brushed upon the skin-charred
Soul, mine
with cathedrals of silk
radiance in wine strong
body that melts off my bones
groaning, fading

—

I rush, push,
an anodyne Hamlet away
yet cannot. I find my tablets
please, please
it is You, Thou
are passing by leaving
only the scent of
memory and
a thing like gossamer scarf
traveling by my cracked lips
please, please
let me grip the hem, hold
forever stagger a lover's
honeyed stagger behind
Thou, in the memory of
You
you . . .

Ambition

How I would trade my soul to be Shakespeare!
How I would hope for mortal gain
Infinite
To sing a sonnet
To pen a psalm.

Wanton Fortune!
Why give me hope but no consummation?
Why give me question, but no -

God, but
there lies the fault, mine.
I sing myself discordant in
Your chorus. Yet still
you call it
Enough.

I sang before for self tangible
so sung in a history never
to matter more than these dead
lines.

Hope, anchor,
whorl me round
Charybdis, away to
the myth in God I am wont
to be.

Burn

In Cincinnati a woman burns
For me, and I
Once desiring
Find yearning a fickle thing.

What feathered pompoms I
Am reduced to tickling
Feather-firm pleasures.

Ah to be at all times the monk
Enraptured by the love of
Sweeping leaves!
To make kisses die in
Nettle bush stings, firm
My grapes
Wine pressed piety.

I will go to
a Cincinnati bed no
more.
Hope
a haggard face, my own
to bed.

Ode to the Gulf of Mexico

Then there was the sea!
Tawdry land, ant-trod earth
in all your majesty of gold-wrought grain waves
from which you've sucked the sea's blood
but are a shadow of her splendor.

To happen in moonless night upon
the sand brushed roar of
Night-swell solitude is
to see, to know
the edge of the world.

What grace is borrowed ours
that we should taste your perfume
feel the warmth of shores kissed
by the sun, you grow fecund
yet by special gift hidden
in the depth all monsters of
your deepest womb.

To love you as I, ape-man
can, you lapping me, I
singing you,
neither overwhelmed.

The Problem of the One and the Many

I.
Was love to be my om?
All words the egg-cracked feathers
which are the bird
the flying
the form
the world
one drip, hazelnut
Love that
interpenetrates other
Ring Dance.

I build my tower of one
monolith word, find
foundations crumble
to speak even the word, cracks
to say, speak, voice
distend my throat
in Babel Babble-

The vertigo of a falling
between love and shattering real
stone, shiver, flesh, variety
ground.

II.
Even the circle word does not hold
the many paths share
that they are paths not
destinations, can
love hold when blood

of martyrs cries out
Christ, in Christ alone!
When you yourself have said
I am way, truth, life?
Few should arrive, save
If you may disguise in other temples and
Be the way in Hindu shrines, — wait

Then who is to say the face I love?
Whisper to, give my life as happy tribute
Is not mere masquerade? Well
There's truth in masks, but
Is it the very fill of truth? Full
Enough? I must confess
You, Christ, my lips have
No other right, nor
Have my lips other good governance.

Can love so personal, hold
When it must break and confess
You different in the world? Have
I the courage to say so? That you
Are an inconstant God? No
Help me
God help me . . .

III.
. . . Then I made the world
A game
Of gifts.

To find the ways to say love and
Let that be my freedom from this.

The truth must be,
And must be true, so

To be so, it must do more
Than talk
It must sing,

and in singing find a rhyme to musty
paradox and the virulent relative. I
am to low to account for it, but I
can give good gifts, first
myself.

Wounds all Heals

Then you'll wake up
someday, look
in the
Mirror
Shadow
so they Doomed

...

Love does not end but
entropies until
one of us is going
to have to
say
Something.

I have been the rat,
first of what might
Might
I have been the captain
gasping out every excuse why we
need one
more, one
more
I have missed the launch of Titanic
Misfortune, scuttled for
something seeming
better The
termite tickling loose bilge
I have been
all
All shadows in
the lines of a mirrored
Face.

Kiss this Page

and so kiss me.

You are the stranger; I've
wanted so long so hard to love
you.

Touch these letters, to touch
me. Explore the goosepimple
chill I feel leaving my ink
scratch caresses.

Listen, listen, place
your ear upon the place your
eyes have traveled again:

these words are in the rhythm of
my heart, their little thrum beating
for you, yes
strange lover I
haven't met.

Theodicies #1

Then God
let it happen yet
looked
on
Weeping, looked
at me.

I was afraid, then.
I knew.
Felt the bone splinter in
Our Brokenness.

I am a man on a floatsam
Cross, tossed
upon the tears which have
made the valley an uncertain ocean.

He knows my feet
touch the valley's lip from
time to time, and take
this as too much more before
the waves come again, and

To live
carried by a tearlogged Cross one
must
lay back
encompass the process
of the stars.

Old Monk

Old Monk sweeps
the soul of the building, no
dust has
settled but it's
nice to hear

Broom swish like
Psalms for days
of sweet Summer's rain.
Here I sojourn with
Spring at night, when
expectation of change can
kill you.

I meet her there, the woman who
smells like smoke on glass and
forgetting. Our
boy flits by, flame flicker life how
it mangles me to see him
fade into half-remembered
pictures, leaves long floating
settle, decay.

God has a seat in
The soul of it all, invite
Him in, sometimes
I know He comes, I
do not pretend an old monk sweeps
anymore, or the woman is
more than desire, or the boy
is not me back then, and

when He comes, I
do not pretend to the reason
why. I simply let
Him in.

A Flower Fairy & a Scarecrow, who Cried

sing us into stars! Place
your tulipped hand upon
this straw chest, kiss
my burlap skin, We
shall laughing watch
the May Pole girls
tell their gay May stories of
our bright pen-pricks of light upon
the sky.

Let us be eternal in
tales richer, other than truth
my blossom-bride, I
your field guard groom,
Father Cowslip we to wed,
field mice to attend the bed,
we shall know little pixies in
your petal womb.

***

We grow old, my
weather-wilt rose I
crow-pecked crone.
The may-pole lies
we worse than dead or forgotten
never-taled.

Come, we will find him.
poet drowsing upon
our wine-strong stars, whisper
our love, sweet
mortal, there once was

The Ring

When you look, see
the swirling ring
dance of me into
you, you into me,
we into other, into
Thee, other all
segment whole, perfect
sphere of light uncreate,
dance.

So you learn for a femto to
step

Perhaps you will step discordant to
the ring of all cause, all other,
with your very soul to see a universe
immoveable and sing it to change
kings, monsters, humans whose
dynamic, perhaps, can choose
to change the tone of
the world.

Or, let the dance take you
Up. Knowing, knowing, no
one is really listening unless
you can somehow
find stillness in the other's soul, which
only comes by their hidden choice
to see you
in the Ring.

You, I am sorry, will
slip back to

the natural view, the silver glass
will dim as you move
without meter, try to dance
unrhythmed shape without
form, speak
about something which
is nothing,
really.

Never forget, the dance
will go on, and
you will find it at
the hour a poem strikes you
unexpected, or a song
sings you anew.
You will know again,
For a moment, before the moment is

Snow in April

Upon the twentieth of
April, the weather
Angels got high
upon the smoke of human rest during
Hard Times.

Laughing, listless, they
troubled father Winter for
a cup of snow to dust my nose.
Winter came up from his
southern rounds to oblige in
the merriment of life.

Father watched on, the
Smile, oh G-d
Smile.
For even angels are given
to the good wild of the earth, lest
they bleed out into
the cool, clear water of
Mytho-poetic concept archetype psycho analogy.
In other words a possession of
human mind.

They Did Not See their Own Beauty

In the men gather
Waffle House in 8am
rain.

The women move to make
hot eggs on a cold plate.
mornin Carlos.
mornin Dave.

In shades of gray the sky
unfolds its birdsong petals
a church bell finds
the day begun.

Silently

I fell in love with you silently, by
feeling the fabric of a church chair
Singing We Three Kings
praying, in prayer
It never occurred to me to doubt
You heard
You heard.
How small you were then
to be able to fit yourself
into my words, how
big you are now
my jaw has broken trying
to say the smallest truth of you.

I stay in love with you silently, in
the scratching of a pen, singing
We Three Kings, praying
in prayer knowing I love
and you being Love
are there.

Muse

Let the poem take you when it may.
Let it be holy wanton
effulgent, sexual
itself a wild conception.
Do not allow yourself the luxury of contraception
stymie through propriety
the product of your seeded brain.
Allowed, always
that better is work
of patient joy, which
loves the order of its fruit-
bearing season, yet!
when the blessed word-giver
comes, put down the book, the work
write her to life, for
all death of life unborn, if anathema
ought to honor idea as well.
So be it a bruised knuckle of an
inconvenient ode, with hair frayed and skirt
torn, let it live!
So in it you may find yourself
alive.

To Write a Work Ex Nihilo

To write a work ex nihilo
from God alone divined
is to win a muse eternal
greater all than earth can find.

To be one incorruptible
so in your kingdom find
Self not of Earthly disrepair
but better stuff comprised.

Sweet honey never could compare
hard steel will never bind
as much as God in poem fair
make beauty my designs.

Love, love is the worker here
and desiring are these lines
for love can make confusion clear
and eterne out simple rhymes.

Surrender

How it irks when
the old words are right!
Full right, full true, I
having stretched out hand and heart
to find my word, my way, I
who like a champion in King James' book-
tavern world venue, ride
to Fairy Queen's Canterbury our
language, I
who like a god of my own microcosm
set out to sing it again, slant
to tell it true, instead
return, again
waterlogged, bruised,
shattered beyond sheepish
to the old, holy house, and
sit upon a quiet pew with God

(silence)

When I to speak, only to say
Blessed he who comes in the name
Lord, mercy
Our Father...

Endearments #1

Sometimes I say I love you by kneeling,
as my Lord like gossamer
strands, smoke procession possession
descends into the place
makes it real.

Sometimes I say I love you by touch
hug to my brother, hand
to my sister, holding and
by holding, hope.

Sometimes I say I love you by
saying it.
The teenage puppy lover in me
shyly whispering sweet floss
to the crack in
the tabernacle
Door.

Machine Myths

I am birthed
Shaking, before mother machine
Naked upon her who is the terror
Of meaningless more.

To find myself the gelding
for pasture, inconsummate for
any homely nipple to
suckle my longing.

How merely the vastness behind
Stars, Scopes, Screens;
they as mythic as ancient monsters
just as real
Information.
Derision,
that vellitous vastness
should be comprehended by
Church words.

Yet I have let the merest pixel
dissolve itself into a world a
word, cast
by the screen dragon which hordes my
Eyes, too
many eyes.

Can I not free Christ, yes
the Word be free,
perhaps, then
Truly, truly, only then
I able to hear him call
Me?

Night Song

When you repose,
compose yourself in Love:
Pray in harmonies
with the angels about you;
some unseen.

Make melodious your life — no
merely attune to
the song of love
you already are.

And should you awake,
shivering in the dischord,
of time too narrow too,
Loud,

Listen, to the heart beaten rhythm
of being, and being,
in itself a very good.
Make nocturnes with the Maker,
chorus with Creator.

Remind your mind of,
itself, a duet divine
(sometimes use lyrics)

Endearments #2

You love like the termite
hidden, laboring, Making
your food the patient
eating away of my wooden ways.

You love like a baker
doting over half-baked cookies like
me, waiting, expectant
for the joy of warmth
to bring me into your indwelling.

You love like a teenage romance, wild
awkward, never
failing, forgetful of
Dignity, poise, about
three seconds from doing something crazy.

You love like dancing, like
rain drop puddle splash prancing
You LOVE, in all the ways I can
think, of and
more after that.

Our Lady of Untying Knots

The heart is a knot
which to all our days
our life is tied.

To loosen, pull,
which may itself more make it tight,
carried in ourselves, jumbled, strained,
by daily jostle, like the rosary
in my pocket, I must
sit with myself most every night
in hope to breathe myself untied.

For a free heart, loose enough to
batten the ship of my longing,
and sail on winds of Grace
to your High Country
I pray.

Mary and Elizabeth

Two women laughing over
full wombs,
pregnant
with the new cosmos...

- touch, twitch
inside kick.
human love in warm deserts, pre-thinking,
pre beheading, before the river,
locusts,
seeking, suckling, for this his
Body,
knit into
the most holy, tender:
place.

Here, all time, all life,
All
in a moment,
to women, wondering,
over expectant wombs.

Memory

The pleasure of a good memory, not
cut with sheepish guilt, nor
abandoned to the wolves of
could have beens, free
from the tyrannic will of mercenary
would and should.
I will do then what I know
now, patient
With an old self, allowing
Was to simply Be.
This is how I would wish, should
I myself remember this moment
in memory.

Chesterton

Apostle to the fay, king
of paradox, he used none
himself. Vast
nimble-minded English
friend of Erin.
Expansive,
he filled a space in me.

For I have sailed to my own island
found my heresy better than
I thought myself, for it not being heresy.
I have stood under once-lamplit
streets, watching
the hammers make themselves
again. I
should preach Christ to
the imps beneath the pumpernickel, first
thanking God, then
among few others,
him.

Alike in Dignity

I.
I am composed of two great houses
Head, and Heart, in strife and love.
Yet in school they were decrying
reign of heart, our passion's land.
Said they like old Adam's keening, "not my mind!
The other part gave sin to me."

My mind is my Adam, heart in Eve alive.
Poor men, who work to chain
the heart like some hysteric thing.
They mistake the heart that looks
to head as call enough
to love only that which heart can give, not
the beautiful giver enough.

Abusive mind, mercenary, forgetful
that Adam and Eve were once,
equal union, no
such chains, so they say
from the passionate Eve, pleased
by fruit that sin
entered in — Mind!
Miserable, wretched, to still
rationalize blame, apportion
away from self, standing silent
eating the fruits of passion's pluck.

II.
Sometimes, washed, clean
my mind echoes Christ, yet

the heart is also Mary's reign.
Would you so say Christ over Mary
casts a silencing dominion
in festal Cana's wedding times?

Second Passion, you are my mother
birthing Second Mind to transcend,
Mind to make the choicest wine
admitted Heart mistakes the Mind at times.

Heart you are the Queen of Heaven
Mind beyond creation finds
God in each, in fullest measure
Peace to parts, love sublime.

Angeline

Turn a light on for me, Angeline,
I know love, I know I can't see.
But in a little while, I'll
be going, so the light
might help, I
don't know, I ain't Lazarus
it's my first time.
Besides, the dark doesn't hide
your crying, I don't need

Keep it off then, save
the sight of me whole for your eyes.
But weak as it is,
weak and so tired
as it is at the limit of my days,
remember my voice, me saying
few things remain in the leaving pain
One that does, always, is
I love you, love, sweet
Angeline.

Poem for a Photo of Two Trees

So the wreath shroud
never loud
growing green makes
a welcome of time's displace.

Old root child, divorced
from lover sky's light, contort
finding yourself a scar
cling to your mother earth
and know the fear of abusive lightning.

Weather-wood, did you self wound? no
you knew
in your secret rood-womb
you were nourishing

life anew
you knew:
green sap would gush erotic, unstymied
in your heart, enshrining
the love that made you strong
enough to risk the sky and find
light, and join the perichoreo
again.

Learning and Growing

Sister, you smile
less than I do, nor
ever have I heard
you laugh without
strong reason.
I have had to learn
your unsmiling is a sign
of the sacred silence you
hold within you,
a holy shushing, too often
to me
always to the world.

Brother, unbothered
as I so often am, by
being aware of the other's being
you, most graciously
sometimes impatiently
remind me that
tonight is your turn
to cook the dinner, so
I must diminish
do the dishes,
give you room in myself
to feed my soul.

The Great Up There

They never wanted heaven.
Never dreamed beyond
moving to the Great Up There.

In the Great Up There,
all my friends and family are waiting
at the gate, everybody
gets in, except
I don't ever have to see anybody
I don't want to.

In the Great Up There
life goes on, but its good
everybody owns their own company
nobody has to work, every
food is the best, nobody
is hungry.

I always do the right choice
I always know the right choice
I am totally free!
In the Great Up There
everybody gets to do everything
equal, unique
no one does anything
to hurt one another.

In the Great Up There
I am a god
I am God!

I live all lifetimes
I know all things
I am still
me?

No, they never wanted heaven, only
themselves, pity
them, they'll never see.

Feeling

Clammed

in my own skin, not
unmindful, not quite
attentive.

Cramped soul
needs to stretch but
shudder snap hot shot
of pain upon the reach to

Buzzed, not on
booze, but like
brittle, dried up raspy
winged fly in the inside
of half-present mind.

Numb, because
some days for no reason
there is no reason, just
a ticking clock of
okay.

Endearments #3

I rarely love in the present:
compose my self, my soul
into act adorable, know
what it is
to fall
asleep on the floor next to
the nearness of you, know
that hand would, could
but maybe never touch
(exposure) is better now
than luxurious aloneness forever.

I have loved, felt
the sting of past ends like cigarette
butts on ghost town streets,
know the wanting of wasting will, would
please, please — I'm sorry, no.

Love is a thing I chase the edges of.
Collecting feathers and eggshells, afraid
in the knowledge that you only gain flying
by leaping all
over again.

Anagnorisis

Just let myself be one unmoved by
losses all to myself having proved,
to strike the sky in fearless, wry,
no more to yearn, a will gone awry

Yet what would it prove,
to be a hard-heart scion?
should I so presume,
should I so move?

Humble/humbled
cuff and crumbled
I am a sloppy kind
of what I wish to be.

You grow tired of this, I
would, too, the sweating
strain to manifest a me on page
who can live with my own
Hypocrisy.

I Hate First Dates

You brought a new color
To my palette, I wanted
To paint you
Into my stars, wanted
To grow tired
Of the way you swallowed
Your food.

Why must I be so
Adept at failing
First impressions?
Being too forward, talking
Too much

I feel too strongly,
Not slowly, not well,
Mistaking sparks for fire
Diving at puddles like an ocean's
Swell.

Should apology washed be offered?
I do better in silence, trusting
You to be the arbiter of your self choosing
W(h)(e)(i)ther I, better tempered
Am worth the time.

Mundus

There are days like a sore throat
soggy toast
boss late wait on a Monday morning.
Days that dribble on in coffee slop
tick-tock tolling clock
stop.
These days amend themselves
to the escape of myself into
the orange peels I just stuffed
into a jacket pocket,
the weekend glass resting
empty of its use upon
the study table;
the universe in plain
particular, making
itself known.

Endearments #4

What impatience awaits your ravishment!
How like a child that should be the fool
shriek I to go again, again
dissolve into a press of giggled cuddles.
how I like a lover, my eyes
dart to the source of your
Word
fondling longing for the scent of your
Inspiration, the touch upon
my tongue of your
Fleshy Grace.
How like a man, and as a man
I compose myself into fantasies that I should die
glorious, heroic, pinned atop you
on a Cross. That all which rots should fall
through the Blood covered, while our dying
sighs mingle upward.
That I should save some small touch of
Thee who saved me.
How like a woman, expansive
in the happy abandon of trust beyond
daggerish eyes, images, into
my secret places and guarded kisses
myself yours, so you mine.

Wherein I Yell at the Future

Why should the ideals exist?
Why draw us on?
Let us, you and I
Talk.
Beyond the contrivances of
well
I see you read this poem
after the 20th century.
So we must have invested
well.
Come now, talk
with me.
Let us find out if the capitalism
Of my day was so very
Important. I
Want you to tell me I'm wrong.
Can you?
Can
You

Saturday Morning

Do you feel it? That
Today will be good.
Will reach out it's gossamer
Strands and kiss your lips
with the fecund notion
of possibility.

That you should be, and being
good. God!

Oh!oh! That I should kiss you!
I, not woman, not man,
Except that you see me to be.
The philosophes be damned,
Let me hold you, you
Hold me.

And that will be enough for a Saturday morning.

St. Anthony, Pray for Us

I'm in an abusive relationship with my inner demons.
(trite, shouts the inner critic, monstrous
remembrances of poetry open mics
open diaries spilled over open
bottles. Because)
even turning on the light
to write this
even the light
was a kind of victory for
Them.
Out of my rhythm.
Out of reasoned reality.
Out.

I imagine the drill to my head
and them escaping like vapor
as it goes deeper, deeper,
except one,
one like a coat check girl,
a ticket on my blended self.

I exorcise that one only through prayer
and perhaps writing the sorts of things
I hate to read, but
should be heard for others
to know sometimes you have to write (and read)
schlubby poems in the dark.

Circle of Fifths

It was music, first
that drew me into
music, a tone that stretched
like a dancer upon the star fretted stage
like a surfer riding the wave into
what? The asking
suggestion, question
luminous perfect sphere of
unafraid unknown
which I slide, sing
scrape upon the surface, watch the ripples.
Is it not right, not true,
to have the hunch that it
embraces me too?

Saints and Mice

Ambrose of Milan (Saint)
was troubled by the mice (common)
who scuttered their way at night
holding hands like palmers do with
the vestry floor.
Troubled, yes, saintly he,
that one grain of His Lord
snatched by servant's starving lips
should fall upon the floor,
become within the realm of the corrupted
rats who brought their filth and disease.

So even saints knew not the whole
of our harmony. That perhaps
a mouse,
a rat, should hear
the sermons of Assisi (Saint), we
might yet learn, one day
how the mice and we
can be united in the Body.
Perhaps
though still so many scurry,
and in Ambrose would wish to clean the host
and the vestry floor
and indeed the mice, so
not to trouble the Mystery
forevermore.

Hello

I think myself too honest in the titles of my poems.
Too honest, yes
with unclenched teeth I try not to trap you
into the suggestion of the deep. I
know well the strength of my beloved language
is within the suggestion, hidden
in a recondition - oh! Isn't
that lovely to pick apart!

My love knows not how to make itself
so playful with you, knows not
the Casanovic charms, flim flam flattery
of little mind nets to tease you into
finding a meaning which pleases you,
myself diminishing to a canvas maze
where you may chart your start and finish
into which portraits of game you choose.
I am not humble enough, nor of the wit
to, writer I, lay down and die
for you.

My lines are the lines upon my face, I
want you to trace them with your hands, want
you to kiss my laughing cheeks, know
the scent of my soul open forever, in the best faith
upon this page.

Church

The building heaves with the voices
expectant, filling, growing full, growing inside
a baby fusses, echoing
against the whish of clothes
the pinpricks of whispers, the
creak of pews
and bones.

There is the sacred in this
pregnant pretense of silence, where
Life bursts at belly seams to
keep quiet, listening
for the church bells and
a new kind of life to begin.

Seventeen

In Appalachia we call them jar flies.
You can hear the rasp of age
need to name reach
life lived in the verdant glow of
discovery, rattle
your jars my brothers and hear
the echoes of Eden.

In my late teens I knew what it was
to shiver, dry
upon my own self in the pretense
of singing
with a girl whose name meant hope
in a language neither of us
spoke.

My love, fresh and wild in its art
of naming Eves
went down to earth to rest, was
consumed by pets
and never knew the relief
of sex.

Upon the turning of 34, I presume
I renew
knowing a second naivete of names
jar flies and dreams
to see about a girl named hope, if only in
language shared.

Mission

Truth holds its court of threads among its counterfeits
them the meaning make in borrowed robes,
who help to weave the quilt,
but are not within
the stitching place.

Unspooled fabric, delicate topography
tapestry manifest of my mind
what little patch histories
we give unto the thing combined.

Yet this fabric remains a scrappable thing
a simple heritage of storylines cut
into the interpretation that lets
us sleep at night, yet

I am pierced by a red-gold thread
which defines upon the corners of me,
God, like a dolphin, leaps
upon the surface of what history has made me,
and dives beneath to anchor me in wanting,
I cross stich myself to Him upon my taken cross
dream of being something like a god —
good, mighty, revered, regarded in gold —
only to realize this blanket, myself
was made for those who are cold.

Theodicy #2

Did Adam know he
was lonely? Had he
with the million lip song speech
for bird and bag and bric-a-brac
find voice to speak of
alone?

(I ask to the tippled church bell,
swing, tweet bird swing bee buzz,
summer jitterbug, who
despite their accompaniment, care
not for me, or do each not thrum
entirely with a love greater than me)

Were there aches in Paradise?
one solitary groan to come from Eden
one lack of love for the little godling;
surely this the greatest spur to your ( )
surely to be alone, made god of a self-formed desolate drift
asteroid spinning, spinning-
is to be mad Provenant to a coffin womb. Hell
that is the oldest love, the oldest thirst of the soul.
Not good, to be alone, the first
Not to grace upon our human stage.
Did Adam and Eve play hide and seek?
Did they flirt with the unknown?

Never Been Good at This

It takes three good-byes to leave my friend's house.
First is the warning, the sense that
the pages, inevitable Calvinists
predestine the sense of ending times.
Should I shudder that this is so often the beginning?
The fearful pin of infinitely guessable probability.
A track mark upon my empirical history. America,
Britain, France, Rome, Like
all good talk, we've said of all
and found ourselves in history.

Then comes the quickening second, allegro
the baby cries, dog bark, sudden upset
which moves us one room closer to
the door. Mindful
we are, and so being, are tired. We
talk of aches and plans and
tomorrows little to-do tracks, cast
about for any

The third is hardest for me, my
I wrote these words to delay you
tug upon your sleeve and whisper
come back, I will miss you, because
there is a great secret in magic, a great
fact that I live within these pages, and though
the hands and eyes that write and type these simple lines
may never see your present gaze, still
I will miss your leaving, when
The pages are all run out.

about the author + photographer

Evan R. Underbrink is a poet, author, and academic in the field
of Theology and the Arts. He has studied at Duke Divinity
School, the University of North Carolina, Boston College,
and Harvard Divinity School. His primary passion is looking
at how art allows us to interact with the divine, deeper reality
of the world and ourselves. He is currently a doctoral student
at the Graduate Theological Union in Berkeley, California.

VITALITY is a circle of friends welcoming all, awakening each other, and reminding each other that we are Whole. Our affordable self-care programs invite everyone to move, to breathe, to rest, to contemplate, to grow...wherever each person begins their self-care journey, wherever and however they want to become.

vitalitycincinnati.org

VITALITY buzz, bliss + books LLC publishes books & creations from VITALITY's circle of friends to inspire love, creativity, + possibility:

A New Setting of the Spiritual Exercises: Hearing, Seeing, Feeling Old Stories in New Ways by the Companions of VITALITY

Selected Homilies: allowing life experience to open up the ways and the Word of God by Richard Bollman, S.J.

yoga is THE ALL: an invitation to sensational life by the Companions of VITALITY

With You in Our Dreams, a reading and coloring book for all ages by Mike Eck (poet) & Claire Long (artist)

Midlife Calm: An Alternative to Midlife Crisis by Krista M. Powers

The Naked Path of Prophet series, including **volume 0** *A Wildly Sensual YAHWEH* by Brian J. Shircliff

vitalitybuzz.org